First World War
and Army of Occupation
War Diary
France, Belgium and Germany

5 DIVISION
Divisional Troops
Divisional Anti-Gas School
1 October 1917 - 30 November 1917

WO95/1539/3

The Naval & Military Press Ltd
www.nmarchive.com
Published in association with The National Archives

Published by

The Naval & Military Press Ltd

Unit 10 Ridgewood Industrial Park,

Uckfield, East Sussex,

TN22 5QE England

Tel: +44 (0) 1825 749494

www.naval-military-press.com

www.nmarchive.com

This diary has been reprinted in facsimile from the original. Any imperfections are inevitably reproduced and the quality may fall short of modern type and cartographic standards.

© **Crown Copyright**
Images reproduced by permission of The National Archives, London, England, 2015.

Contents

Document type	Place/Title	Date From	Date To
Heading	WO95/1539/3		
Heading	5th Division 5th Arty Gas School 1917 Oct-1917 Nov		
Heading	War Diary of 5th Divisional Anti-Gas School For Month Of October 1917		
War Diary	Field	01/10/1917	31/10/1917
Miscellaneous	Received From 23rd D.G.O the following Stores	02/10/1917	02/10/1917
Miscellaneous	Issued to 14th Div Gas Officer	15/10/1917	15/10/1917
Miscellaneous	Issued to 7th Divl Gas Officer	18/10/1917	18/10/1917
Miscellaneous	List Of Gas Stores In Divisional Area	23/10/1917	23/10/1917
Miscellaneous	List Of Stores issued to Chemical Advised Xth Corps	29/10/1917	29/10/1917
Heading	War Diary of 5th Divisional Anti-Gas School For Month Of November 1917.		
War Diary	Field	01/11/1917	30/11/1917

WO 95/15391

5th Division

5th Anti Gas School

~~October November~~

~~1917~~

(ITALY)
1917 OCT ———— 1917 NOV

War Diary
of
5th Divisional Anti-Gas School
for
Month of October 1917.

[signature]
Captain. R.E.
Div. Gas Officer.

Army Form C. 2118.

WAR DIARY
or
INTELLIGENCE SUMMARY. 5th Divisional Anti Gas School
(Erase heading not required.)

Instructions regarding War Diaries and Intelligence Summaries are contained in F. S. Regs., Part II. and the Staff Manual respectively. Title pages will be prepared in manuscript.

Place	Date	Hour	Summary of Events and Information	Remarks and references to Appendices
Field	1.10.17		D.G.O. accompanied by D.G.O. 23rd Divn visited Gun position of a battery which had been heavily shelled with "Mustard Gas" shells. Many casualties were due to lack of training and an insufficient knowledge of the dangerous effects of the Gas in question. Reports were sent to C.R.A. and C.R.A. The battery "gassed" was one of the D. of L.	See Appendix 1.
	2.10.17		23rd Divl Anti-gas school moved to Berthen and we took possession of the vacated premises. Day spent in re-arranging Stores and "Billets"	
	3.10.17		Routine work carried out by the Bde N.C.O.s. N.C.O. at Stores took over duties at school, and N.C.O. at school went to Stores (Both R.O.S).	
	4.10.17		D.G.O. reported to D.H.Q. and visited 95th Bde HQs. Officers, N.C.O.s & men of No 2 by Team were instructed and drilled, and tested thru Lr Ro in Gas at the School. Wonting book by N.C.O.s	
	5.10.17 to 6.10.17		D.G.O. visited various C.C.S. re "Gassed Cases". C.C.A. visited school re Gas shelling in the Area. 12.30 pm H. Marson, 16th RWK left school for England to take a commission in the R.F.C.	
	7.10.17		Stores at D.A.D.O.S. moved by lorry from Bonninghelst to Ouest Centre. D.G.O. visited C.C.A. Routine work by Bde Gas NCOs	
	8.10.17		D.G.O. rptd to D.H.Q. and visited 13th Bde HQ. Brigade Gas NCOs rptd at school and received instructions regarding the placing of Strombos Horns.	
	9.10.17 to 12.10.17		D.G.O. suffering from effects of "O.H." Visited C.C.S. but refused to stay there. Tried to select N.C.O.s of C.C.A and B.B.G.Os. of 14th & 139th Regts. Strombos Horn placed at Woodcote House. Special attention paid to "drafts" by Bde N.C.O.s.	
	13.10.17		D.G.O. rptd to D.H.Q. and visited 16th R.W.K. re condition of R.B.Ros. Bde Gas NCOs rptd to school.	

Army Form C. 2118.

WAR DIARY or INTELLIGENCE SUMMARY.

(Erase heading not required.)

5th Divis'l Anti-Gas School

Place	Date	Hour	Summary of Events and Information	Remarks and references to Appendices
Field	14.10.17		100 Blankets for Eng: nets arrived. N.C.O.s prepared them in readiness for issue to the Artillery.	
	15.10.17		D.G.O. visited D.H.Q. re classes. Further work in dipping blankets. 15th Bde. R.F.A. drew 20. D.G.O. visited Electro and Corps Reinforcement Camp. Arrangements made for a N.C.O. to assist Corps. C.C.A. visited school.	See Appendix 2.
	16.10.17		D.G.O. visited 12 Howitzers & 1st S. Surreys. Six N.C.Os assisted 14th D.G.O. in training of 2nd Batt. 2212 Bde. A.I.F. Routine work by Bde. N.C.Os	
	17.10.17		D.G.O. interviewed two officers desirous of being transferred to I.S. Bde N.C.Os reptd on condition of S.B.R.s after the recent action operations. 4 N.C.O reptd to Reinforcement Camp for instruction. 16th Rifle Bde reptd to D.G.O. for duty as batman.	
	18.10.17 to 20.10.17		An Sw't Artillery had been rather heavily gas shelled, D.G.O and C.C.A. visited H.A.R.F.A. and the shelled areas, to give any advice and assistance necessary. Specimen of "Yellow Cross" shells were obtained and forwarded to G.H.Q. Details reports were sent to G.S.O.III and C.C.A. Routine work was carried out by the N.C.Os and visits paid them S.B.R.s to gas at the school	See Appendix 3.
	21.10.17		Reports of work sent to G.S.O.III and C.C.A. A N.C.O at Corps Reinforcement Camp. Bde Gas N.C.Os reptd to D. G.O.	
	22.10.17		D.G.O. visited gun position on Hill 60 and obtained another specimen of Yellow Cross Gas shell. This was forwarded to Corps. Routine work by Bde N.C.Os.	
	23.10.17 to 25.10.17		D.G.O. reptd to R.A.O. and visited 15th, 13th & 95th Bde H.Q. Received Gas stores from 110th Div. Routine work by N.C.Os attached to Bdes.	See Appendix 4.
	26.10.17		D.G.O visited C.C.A. and received visit from 39th D.G.O. Application from Corps for a N.C.O. Sgt Roberts recommended. N.C.O. at Reinforcement Camp.	

Army Form C. 2118.

WAR DIARY
or
INTELLIGENCE SUMMARY.
(Erase heading not required.)

5th Divis'l Anti-Gas School

Instructions regarding War Diaries and Intelligence Summaries are contained in F. S. Regs., Part II. and the Staff Manual respectively. Title pages will be prepared in manuscript.

Place	Date	Hour	Summary of Events and Information	Remarks and references to Appendices
Field	14.10.17		100 Blankets for Dug-outs arrived. N.C.O.s "prepared" them in readiness for issue to the Artillery. D.G.O. visited D.H.Q. re classes.	
	15.10.17		Further work in defining Blankets. 15th Bde R.F.A. drew 20. D.G.O. visited Glosters and Corps Reinforcement Camp. Arrangements made for a N.C.O. to assist Corps. C.C.A. visited school.	See Appendix 2.
	16.10.17		D.G.O. visited 12 Glosters & 1st E. Surreys. Two N.C.Os assisted 14th D.G.O. in training of 2nd Batt. 2&2 Bde A.H. Routine work by Bde N.C.Os.	
	17.10.17		D.G.O. interviewed two officers desirous of being transferred to G.S. Bde N.C.Os rept on condition of S.B.R.s after the recent Actor operations. D.G.O. reptd to Reinforcement Camp for Westminsters. 16th R.W.K. reptd to D.G.O. for duty as batman.	
	18.10.17 to 20.10.17		As 2nd Army Artillery had been rather heavily gas shelled, D.G.O. and C.C.A. visited H.Q. R.F.A. and the shelled Zones to give any advice and assistance necessary. Specimens of "Yellow Cross" shells were obtained and forwarded to G.H.Q. Details reports were sent to G.S.O. III and C.C.Q. Routine work was carried out by Gas N.C.Os and Units tested their S.B.R.s as g.o. at the school.	See Appendix 3.
	21.10.17		Reports of work sent to G.S.O. III and C.C.A. A N.C.O. at Corps Reinforcement Camp. Box Gas N.C.Os reptd to D.G.O.	
	22.10.17		D.G.O. visited gun positions on Hill 60 and obtained another specimen of Yellow Cross Gas Shell. This was forwarded to Corps. Routine work by Bde N.C.Os.	
	23.10.17 to 25.10.17		D.G.O. reptd to R.F.A. and visited 13th, 15th & 95th Bde Hd. Received Gas stores from 14th Div. Routine work by N.C.Os attached to Bdes.	See Appendix 4.
	26.10.17		D.G.O. visited C.C.A. and received visit from 39th D.G.O. Application from Corps for a N.C.O. for batted recommended. N.C.O. at Reinforcement Camp.	

Army Form C. 2118.

WAR DIARY
or
INTELLIGENCE=SUMMARY. 5th Divisional Anti-Gas School

(Erase heading not required.)

Place	Date	Hour	Summary of Events and Information	Remarks and references to Appendices
Field	29.10.17 to 29.10.17		D.G.O. with A.D.M.S. visits each day to Artillery positions subjected to Gas-shelling, and reports sent in of all "Gas shoots" in divisional area. Alert given to one battery to temporarily abandon the gun positions until the gas disperses. The shelled areas have been treated with Chloride of Lime, this treatment has not been successful owing to the continuous shelling of the treated areas. Sgt Kendrick, 15th D.W.R. leaves school for 2nd Army Gas Course.	See Appendix 5
	30.10.17 to 31.10.17		D.G.O. visits Artillery positions and advanced dressing stations. Box Gas Nets at advanced Hdqtrs. 100 Blankets for Reg-mts. arrive. N.C.O. "prepares" these in readiness for issue.	

Appendix 1

**ANTI-GAS SCHOOL,
5TH DIVISION.**
No.....
Date 2.10.17

Received from 23rd D.G.O the following Stores

Ayrton Fans	140
Rattles	29
Strombos Horns	4
Cylinders (Air)	20
Vacuum Balls	96
Vermorel Sprayers	2
Blankets G.S.	20
Cylinders (Blue Star)	3
Cylinders (Red Star)	4
Cylinders (White Star)	4
P. Bombs	160
M.S.K. Grenades	48
Smoke Candles	15

B.H.Tanywell (for D.G.O)
Lm.

Appendix 2.

> ANTI-GAS SCHOOL,
> 5TH DIVISION.
>
> No. ....
> Date 15.10.17

Issued to 14th Div: Gas Officers the following stores:-

Fans	100
Stromboo Horns	2
Rattles	29
Blankets	50
Air Cylinders	12

B.H. Langwell Lt.
for D.G.O.

Appendix 3

ANTI-GAS SCHOOL,
5TH DIVISION.
No.................
Date 15.10.17

Issued to 7th Divl. Gas Officer the
undermentioned Stores:-

 "P" Grenades   6
 M.S.K Grenades   3
 Smoke Cases   3

     B.H. Langwell Lt.
      for D.G.O.

Appendix 4.

**ANTI-GAS SCHOOL,
5TH DIVISION.**

No. ....
Date 23/10/17

List of "Gas Stores" in Divisional Area, taken over from 14th Divn, on relief.

Horns Strombos	4
Cylinders Air	26
Hans Anti-gas	100
Rattles	48

B H Langwell Lt.
for D.G.O

Appendix 5.

ANTI-GAS SCHOOL, 5TH DIVISION.
No.
Date 29.10.17

List of Stores issued to Chemical Advisers Xth Corps.

Cylinder (Blue Star)	1
Cylinder (Red Star)	2
M.S.K. Bombs	36
P. Bombs	36

B H Langwell 2/Lt.
for D.G.O.

War Diary
of
5th Divisional Anti-Gas School.
for
Month of November 1917.

[signature]
Captain
Div. Gas Officer.

Army Form C. 2118.

WAR DIARY
or
INTELLIGENCE SUMMARY
(Erase heading not required.)

5th Divl Anti-gas School

Instructions regarding War Diaries and Intelligence Summaries are contained in F.S. Regs., Part II. and the Staff Manual respectively. Title pages will be prepared in manuscript.

Place	Date	Hour	Summary of Events and Information	Remarks and references to Appendices
Field	1.11.17 to 4.11.17		Divisional Gas Officer visited Brigade H.Q. and various batteries in action to investigate reported Gas shell bombardments. Reports sent to G.S.O. II and C.C.A. One damaged Gas N.C.O. sent to Base Depots (for six). Routine work at school and stores by N.C.Os. Blanket protection to superintend.	
	5.11.17 to 7.11.17		D.G.O. visited Wardrecli House and Divl Laundry to inspect clothing affected by H.S. Sgt Roddick returned from 2nd Army Gas School. Routine work by Divl Gas N.C.Os.	
	8.11.17		D.G.O. proceeded to England on leave. Sgt Newton reported to 1/c A.S.H. and Div H.Q.	
	9.11.17 to 11.11.17		Routine work at school and stores. Visit of C.C.A. and 39th D.G.O. to school. Area stores handed over to 39th D.G.O. Sgt Roddick left school to take up duties as instructor at 10th Corps Gas School.	
	12.11.17 to 13.11.17		School stores and equipment packed up and despatched to Ordnance. 39th D.G.O. takes over remainder of stores at school. Sgt Newton proceeded to XII Corps Gas School, to take up duties as instructor.	
	14.11.17		Move from Rennghelst to Nielles-les-Bleguin.	
	15.11.17 to 17.11.17		Arrangement of stores and taking over of billets for staff. Reports sent to D.A.A. and C.C.A. as to location of school.	
	18.11.17		Rest of C.C.A. re-instruction of troops whilst in rest. Instructions as to training, sent to Base Gas N.C.Os.	
	19.11.17 to 21.11.17		Routine work by Divl Gas N.C.Os. No.16903 Sgt Hodgetts F.A. 15th R.W.R. reported at School. Instructions given to him as to the training of his Bde.	
	22.11.17		Pte Woodward proceeded to England on leave. Divl Gas N.C.Os reported to School. Routine work.	
	23.11.17		Capt. Greenwood returned from leave. Routine work by Divl Gas N.C.Os.	
	24.11.17		Wire sent for Pte Woodward to return from leave. Stores and equipment packed up ready to move.	
	25.11.17		Move from Nielles-les-Bleguin to Herdin.	
	26.11.17 to 30.11.17		Arrangement of stores. Capt. Greenwood reported to D.A.Q. giving location of Units. Visits to Central Laboratory. Routine work by Bde N.C.Os. Refitting of Units.	

A. Newitt
Capt.
D.G.O.